TOURING FRANCE WITH THE HONDA S2000

By Chris Bradley

PREFACE

For those of you not yet an aficionado of the Honda S2000 I expect you will be asking the question 'Why a Honda S2000?' And for all intents and purposes, it could well have been any other car, or even a motorhome for that matter, except, I just happen to own a Honda S2000.

Launched in 1999 to celebrate Honda's 50th Anniversary (1950-2000) TheS2000 is nothing less than a racing car. Boasting a red line of an incredible 9000 RPM and delivering the highest horsepower per litre of any normally aspirated engine in the world at the time. Power was achieved by Honda's revolutionary Vtec (variable valve timing system). However, it suffers from a lack of torque at lower revs and only excels at between 7000 & 9000 rpm. Like I said, a racing car; making it great for the Nürburgring but big trouble if you try driving it to its potential on the streets, as many have found out to their peril. Combine all that with typical Japanese reliability and you really-need go no further. However, Honda did go further and there is a list of characteristics they added that derived directly from Honda's Formula 1 racing pedigree, making the Honda S2000 a unique and very special sports car. Apart from that, Honda don't make them anymore. After production ceased in 2009, it was almost certainly destined to become a future classic. Here's hoping!

The Honda S2000 is of course no Aston Martin or Ferrari, however, it's still great for the following three reasons: - Fast, Cheap and Reliable. Usually you only get two out of the three. It also still looks great even 17 years on. They have a huge following in the USA and the S2000 featured in the very first Fast and Furious movie.

PLANNING – *in the rough*

We chose Portsmouth from where to make the crossing to France and where Brittany Ferries would deliver us some way further south in Normandy to the town of Caen. An early embarkation meant we needed to plan a stay over somewhere near to Portsmouth and I spotted a good offer on Booking.com for the Langstone Hotel on Hayling Island. Next, we wanted to establish a base somewhere near Bordeaux where we could explore the surrounding area and the Dordogne, maximizing our time for sightseeing but also giving us time to relax around a pool and enjoy some of that French cheese and red wine we hear about.   Once we had made our choice of Gite it was then simply a question of joining up the dots between hotels and Chateau's, placing them not more than about 100 miles apart and taking in some of the places we had earmarked to visit along the way.

Our last night in France would be spent in Versailles where we purchased tickets to see the Fountains and Fireworks display, so we needed to plan to depart from Le Havre late in the afternoon. We would then make our way back to Portsmouth and yet another night at the Langstone Hotel on Hayling Island before our trip North and home.

LEGS

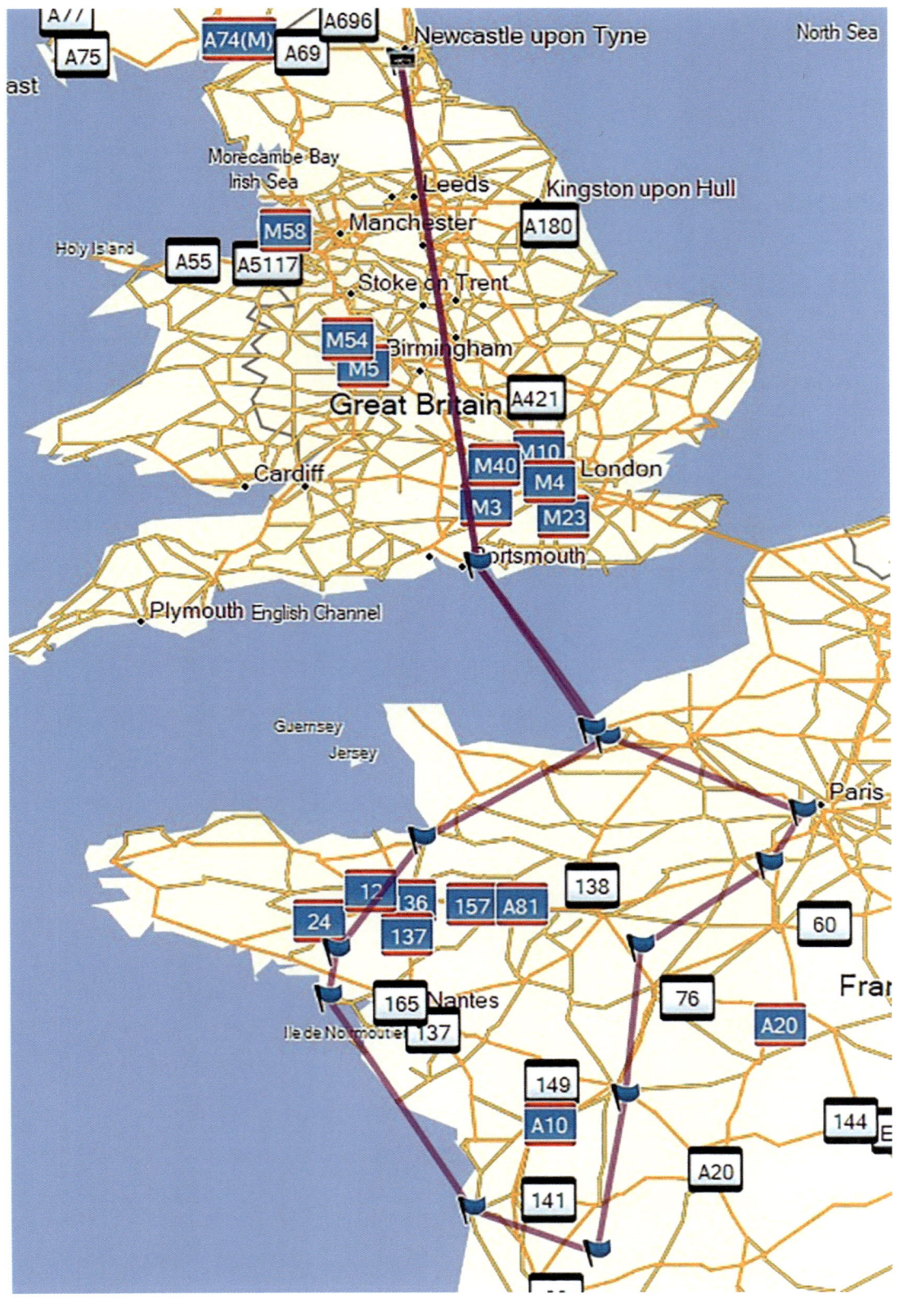

STOPS ALONG THE WAY

- Hayling Island
- Honfleur
- Mont St Michel
- Guerande
- Royan
- Saint Romain (5 nights)
- Beauvoir
- La Chartre-sur-le-Loir
- Denonville
- Versailles
- Hayling Island

DRIVING IN FRANCE

Driving in France requires several special considerations. Apart from having to drive on the right there are different laws regarding equipment you need to carry which do not apply in the UK. For instance: - First Aid Kit, Reflective Triangle, Hi viz jackets for all passengers, Two breathalyzer's, Spare Spectacles and a Spare bulb kit. A GB sticker and headlight deflectors are also obligatory although night driving was not in our plan. For anyone planning to drive in Cities you will also need an Air Quality Service Certificate. Designed to help reduce pollution within cities. Available on line at the following address: - https://www.certificat-air.gouv.fr/en/

The Air Quality Certificate is a secure sticker that goes in the windscreen of the vehicle and indicates its environmental class according to its emissions of air pollutants.

There are 6 classes of certificates. The air quality certificate helps to favour the least polluting vehicles:

- Favourable parking arrangements;
- Preferred traffic conditions;
- In restricted traffic areas (ZCR) or in the event of a pollution peak.

The air quality certificate is mandatory to Drive in the restricted zones established by certain local authorities, or when restrictions are enforced during certain periods of high pollution.

My Honda S2000 is classed as **Euro 3 -** All new vehicles from January 2000

You will need your V5 log book at hand when applying and the cost is €4.8 at the time of writing. Certificate is shown on the next page and a sticker is supplied for the windscreen.

Toll Roads

A lot of the A class motorways in France demand tolls. You can pay at the end of each leg or you can obtain a device which you attach to your windscreen that monitors your use and charges are made to your credit card automatically. More info here: - http://www.drive-france.com/faqs/tolls-france/ Special lanes allow a faster transition through each checkpoint.

Service de délivrance des Certificats Qualité de l'Air

Imprimerie nationale S.A. - Opérateur de services en application du décret n° 2015-886 du 15 juillet 2015
Société Anonyme au capital de 34 500 000€ - Siège social : 104 avenue du président KENNEDY 75016 PARIS
SIREN : 352.973.622 RCS PARIS - SIRET : 352.973.622.00181 - TVA Intracommunautaire . FR.08.352.973.622
Code APE : 1812.Z

FACTURE

N° Dossier : 17 1434 3771 2803

N° : 1704621018

Christopher Bradley

Address

ROYAUME-UNI

Date facture : 25/05/2017
Date d'échéance : 25/05/2017

Description	Qté	P.U. HT	Montant HT	
Certificat Qualité de l'Air	1	3,08 €	3,08 €	(1)
Affranchissement	1	1,10 €	1,10 €	(2)

FACTURE ACQUITTEE par   CB
pour   W791ALA

	Total H.T. (EUR)	Total TVA (EUR)	Total T.T.C. (EUR)
(1) 20.0 %	3,08 €	0,62 €	3,70 €
(2) 0.0 %	1,10 €	0,00 €	1,10 €
			4,80 €

Facture numéro :	1704621018	VIREMENTS FRANCE sur notre compte :
Date :	25/05/2017	SOCIETE GENERALE PARIS
N° Dossier :	17 1434 3771 2803	IBAN : FR76 3000 3030 1000 0201 9443 195
		BIC : SOGEFRPP
Montant de la facture :	4,80 €	TVA SUR LES DEBITS

le coupon ci-dessous peut être utilisé comme justificatif provisoire de classement du véhicule dans l'attente de la réception du Certificat qualité de l'air par courrier.

W791ALA

Pour toute information, contactez notre centre de gestion - Tél. 0 800 97 00 33 (Service & appel gratuits) -
Courriel : contact@certificat-air.gouv.fr

*

DRIVING IN FRANCE

You will need to take the following documents with you when you go to France.

- Vehicle Log book V5
- Insurance Certificate
- Insurance Green Card (A slip of paper showing that you are insured for driving in France)
- Current MOT certificate

Then the obvious...

- Tickets
- Passport
- Money

OTHER CONSIDERATIONS

If you need car parking, make sure you contact the hotel where you are staying in advance just in case.

USEFUL TELEPHONE NUMBERS

112 - European general emergency number

15 - Medical emergency/accidents/ambulance

17 - Police or Gendarmerie

18 - Fire brigade

PREPARATION

Preparing the Honda meant a full overhaul of the brake calipers which were overdue for a service and to compliment the newly refurbished wheels and tyres, new disc rotors and pads were installed. Valve clearances checked and oil and filter changed. An MOT was due in May and this confirmed the car was in sound condition for the long journey. Bridgestone Potenza RE050 A's are my choice of tyre. Wheel alignment had been done in 2016.

PREPARATION

Honda S2000. 2.0 litre 16v – V-tec - 237bhp - 150mph 0-60 - 6 seconds   1999 – 2009

Thank goodness, the Honda has a proper boot, or trunk if you live in the USA. It's not uncommon to find the drop-down roofs on some roadsters occupies most of the space otherwise allocated for luggage. That's OK for zipping around town, but not so good if your planning to tour for several weeks. That said, we still had to manage the space we did have wisely to get everything in we *absolutely* needed. This included a comprehensive tool kit in case of emergencies and a litre of engine oil. Dumping the old 6 cd autochanger and fitting a new Pioneer stereo unit that Blue- toothed to my phone for both music and telephone calls, freed up some more valuable space, while at the same time still giving me access to my Chuck Berry collection. I'm sure you know where I am coming from here!

Day 1

On the morning of 18th June 2017 with everything stowed, I looked at my watch and were ready to go at 09.00. The BBC Weather Forecast predicted fine weather, it was probably the best day for fine weather in the North East of England since records began. I pulled the Honda out of the garage and noticed the radio was switched off and when attempting to switch it back on again realised there was no power to the set. The previous night I had decided to try out my newly purchased electric tyre inflator and put some more air into the rear tyre's to compensate for the extra weight of luggage. After doing one tyre the thing stopped working. There appeared to be no power to the pump. I naturally assumed the pump had failed so I hastily arranged its return to Amazon and managed to order up a new one to be collected from Screwfix that morning. As it turned out No 5 fuse under the dash had blown. For some reason the radio and auxiliary were on the same 10amp fuse. The inflator needed a 15amp fuse. So, the first stop of our journey was to be Screwfix, Gateshead.

The drive down country was long and laborious although the fine weather made driving the Honda a pleasant experience, as it always did with the roof down and cruising at around 63mph, just keeping us ahead of the lorries. Eventually, on joining the M25 I was alerted to the fact that an accident between junction14 and junction 16 was causing severe delays and the exit to join the M3 was completely closed, just exactly where we were headed. After crawling in traffic for some time we detoured off via the M4 and explored Surry for a while before joining the M3 further West.

The delay set us back about two hours and we didn't arrive at our hotel on Hayling Island until about 18.30 but happy to have completed that first long leg of the journey safely, and on such a lovely day. The Langstone Hotel turned out to be a good stopping off point for Portsmouth with probably the best location I have ever encountered in my forty years travelling the UK. The Sun set perfectly over a tranquil glistening sea adorned by a multitude of sailing yachts anchored to their moorings.

The bridge crossing to Hayling Island

Day 2

Day two began with an early breakfast followed by a short drive to the ferry terminal. Its surprisingly easy to access the Brittany ferry port from the highway and we were soon on board the vessel Normandie. Although I had booked a cabin just in case my wife needed to lie down if the crossing had been a rough one, or if there was a shortage of seating, as we had often encountered on trips across the Irish Sea to the Isle of Man. In fact, it turned out that we didn't use the cabin at all as the sea was calm, the Sun shone as it had the previous day and there was plenty room on the Normandie to sit in both the lounge areas and in the restaurants.

As we left the terminal at Portsmouth we could look across at the Royal Naval Yard and see HMS Victory just beyond. It was heartwarming somehow to be reminded of our great naval heritage although sadly HMS Victory looked quite depleted and bare without her masts and rigging. We passed the famous Spinnaker Tower and finally out to sea.

Normandie

  Life aboard ship was quite pleasant and I was able to take time to play with google translate and even tried to practice some of my modest French on an assistant at the coffee shop. Either she didn't hear me or she was just totally unimpressed by my lame attempt and didn't bother to respond, leaving me with a few doubts as to my limited vocabulary. C'est la vie.

  One of my anxieties about the trip was that I would be driving on the right in a right-hand drive car. I have driven abroad before several times but always in a left hand-drive vehicle. Surprisingly, the drive off the ferry and onto the highway was straight forward and in fact, it felt more natural than if I were in the left seat. I suppose the controls of the S2000 are all very familiar to me.

  Travelling North and following the coastal rout as best we could towards our first hotel, we passed via Carbourg, which is just North of Le Havre and were amazed by the beautiful sandy beaches and promenade there. The beaches are overlooked by holiday homes with delightful architecture, including a thatched cottage where we watched a workman busy renewing the roof. The weather was still with us so the beaches looked a whole lot more inviting than they probably did in 1943.

Carbourg

Carbourg

The drive to our hotel also took us along by the harbour in Hornfleur. The harbour ranks very highly as one of the most picturesque harbours I have seen and certainly on a par with those I have seen in Holland. Restaurant canopies and parasols skirt almost every inch of the harbour and the narrow back lanes that lead off from the harbour into the town have a treasury of interesting shops for the tourist, selling wonderful delicacies such as pastries, nougat, dried fruits and chocolate. Everything you don't need if you are watching your weight.

   That evening we chose a restaurant in the market square to eat, away from the bustle of the waterside where we met a very nice couple from Toulouse who helped us with translation.

   Happily we were able to order a meal on our first night in France without too much trouble. During the conversation, I was asked about our trip and when the man found out we were touring in an S2000 he was extremely pleased to tell me everything he knew about the car and even downloaded an image onto his mobile phone to show his girlfriend. I, of course felt extremely chuffed.

As we finished our main course and the last of the French Fries and at just after 9.30pm the bells from a tower next to St Catherin's Church in the square erupted. I was not sure if it was bell practice but we were all quite amused by the two bells which went on and on as the bell ringer persevered, eventually stopping in a gradual and fading conclusion to his efforts. Fortuitously for us, just in time for dessert. Thank goodness. You can't get much of a tune out of two bells!

   After our meal, and now rendered partially deaf by the bells, we had a final walk along the harbour wall and around the town then headed back to our hotel, just a few Kilometers out of town. In every case I chose to book a hotel where we would be able to park the Honda off road and not using public car parking, which can so often happen if you choose a hotel in a town. You see the French don't have the same love affair of their cars in quite the same way as we British do. So, I was forever concerned I would come down in the morning to find dents in every panel.

A fish restaurant in Honfleur

Hornfleur harbour

Day 3

Our first whole day in France began with a visit to Caen and William The Conquerors Castle. I set the Sat-Nav for Caen. I knew the castle was in the center of town and so the navigator would get me close enough to be able to pick up the tourist road signs. When you arrive at the castle you will see signs for the Castle parking where you will be directed to an underground car park. I decided to try and find something outside and close to the castle wall. I drove a few yards further up the road where there I found some roadside parking and put the Honda on a meter.

William the Conquerors castle is no more than a ruin today but it has now also been embellished by a museum and small church. The castle wall and ramparts were quite something to see and you can imagine the moat when it would have been filled with water. To get the full story of William's rise to power and eventual victory over Harold Godwinson at the famous battle of 1066 you must travel to Bayeaux and see the Tapestry, so this was to be our next port of call.

Arriving in Bayeaux we passed by a war memorial and graveyard on the edge of town, of which there are many in Normandy. Sadly, we did not have enough time for a visit and headed directly down into the town itself. Bayeaux is breathtakingly beautiful. We found parking just off the delightful main street and not far from tapestry building which is located about 100 meters on the other side. The museum is well signposted from there.

If you are really interested in the events that led up to the famous battle of 1066, I recommend you read "1066 The year of the three battles" by Frank Mclynn. It recounts detail about Harold Siggurdson (Hardrader) of Norway, who's story is quite fascinating and how he was courted by Harold's brother Tostig to invade England from the North where he subsequently sacked York. Godwinson's army marched North and defeated Hardrader at Stamford Bridge but then had to quickly return to stem Williams invasion in the South. If Godwinson had only waited a few days for reinforcements to arrive the outcome of the battle may have been totally different. After that day, England was to change, and under Norman we see the building of Cathedrals, Churches and castles throughout the land.

As I stood outside the Museo in Bayeaux my attention was drawn to a Ferrari 285 that pulled into the car parking area, closely followed by a Honda S2000 AP1. Hoping to have a chat with the drivers my wife volunteered that we were also there in our Honda S2000 and that set the course for the rest of the conversation, albeit brief. Comforted in the fact that I was not the only one touring in France with a Honda S2000, I was also disappointed I was not the only ONE touring France in a Honda S2000. If you get my meaning?   However, this was not to be the last time we came across another Honda S2000, nor its notoriety, on our continuing journey.

William The Conquerors Castle, Caen

An old watermill just off the main street

Bayeaux Cathedral

Satisfied that I was now an expert on the Norman Invasion of England, albeit very disappointed I was not able to take photographs of the tapestry, my attention was refocused on the Geordie invasion of France, our next overnight stop and Mont Saint Michel.

I have seen many photographs if Mont Saint Michel, taken both by day and at night, but nothing can prepare you for the real thing. We had made good time in the morning so decided to check in to our lodgings, fuel up the Honda and head straight for the Mont. We arrived at our B+B in Beauvoir which was within walking distance of the town itself and we were warmly greeted by our host designate and given the keys to our room. Then set off for the mount.

There are several ways to reach the Mont St Michel. Walk, Swim, Horseback, Beach Buggy, etc. etc. But most people drive to the car park and get a free bus shuttle that ferries you across the causeway and back for a meagre €12 at the time of writing. This included car park and shuttle. Inside the outer wall there is great exploring to be had, especially if you buy a ticket to visit the Abbey and see the many vast halls, chapels and cloisters that have been cleverly constructed over several levels on the Mont. The street, and there is only one, is filled with bars, restaurants and gift shops but everything seems to carry a premium so taking your own food and drink could save you some euro's.

Two Icons of Historical Interest….. Three if you count my wife!

Mont Saint Michel

The main street Inside Mont Saint Michel which eventually leads up to the Abbey.

One of the several chambers inside the Abbey

The Spire of Mont St Michel

The man powered winch used to raise goods up to the Abbey on a sledge

Looking towards the mainland

A view from the fortified turret.

Near the entrance to the Abbey

   On returning to our accommodation, Chambres d'Hotes les vieilles Digues, we sat down in the garden and shared some Rose Wine with the owner Danielle, whom I now think of affectionately as Madame Beauvoir. That evening we walked along to the nearest restaurant in town and enjoyed a great steak, along with the obligatory French Fries, and there, struck up a conversation with a couple from the UK who had a motorhome parked on a nearby site. Keeping contact with Brits seemed to have the effect of boosting our confidence somehow.

   Back at our lodgings I finished the evening with a couple of beers which I had previously put in the communal fridge for a special occasion. Night two in France! Yes!

Day 4

Breakfast started at a little past 08.30 and Danielle (Madam Beauvoir) impressed us with her homemade cakes pastries and jam. We ate and ate. Unfortunately, we had our fill while Danielle was still bringing yet more delicious food into the breakfast room. Her late start at preparing breakfast, she admits apologetically, is quite normal. Lesson learned!

Our next leg of the journey, Beauvoir to Guerande would be broken by a visit to the village of Rochefort En Terre. A place I had read about in magazines and realising it would be a small detour from our route had to include it on the itinerary.

Note

Before setting off for France I made myself a rule that I would top the fuel tank up at the first filling station we came across after the segments on the fuel gauge got down to half way, not knowing where we would be when we needed fuel. The fuel gauge was below half way so stopped at a motorway services on route to Rochefort En Terre and there, while I was standing at the pump, didn't a Honda S2000 scream past and park up in front of the forecourt shop. Same year as my S2000. It turned out the owner had been gifted the car by his now deceased uncle and he had spent a lot of time refurbishing it to its present pristine state. The two cars were photographed side by side like a pair of silver twins. Same year, same colour.

This was now the second Honda S2000 we had come across. I wondered when we would encounter the next Honda S2000 in France?

Matching Colour & Year

The Creperie in Rochefort en Terre

Rochefort en Terre must be one of the prettiest of French villages and when we were there in mid-June the village was filled with the colours of flowers in bloom. We quickly found a delightful Creperie with a rear outside garden and there devoured our second meal of the day, this time served with Chantilly Cream. Oh Dear! Don't come to France expecting to lose weight!

Surprisingly you can drive a car right through the village, so I was not about to miss an opportunity for a photo call with the Honda center stage. The village has a hotel located in town and an old Chateau which is a pleasant walk up the hill from the car park, where you can look over the rooftops of the village from the old battlements.

The main street Rochefort en Terre

Rochefort en Terre

Part of The Chateau at Rochefort en Terre

The main Street Rochefort en Terre

A French Doorstep in Rochefort en Terre

Our journey continued along excellent French tarmac and there were several places where I just had to stop the Honda and take photographs. Brittany is a very beautiful part of France and not dissimilar to England in many ways. Hardly surprising a lot of British Ex Pats live there.

Finally, we reached Guerande, and although I had chosen a Best Western hotel just off the outer ring road (car Parking) we drove straight into town and circumnavigated the medieval city wall just to get our bearings and a feel for the town.

Guerande is a medieval walled fortress town located close to the coast. Unfortunately, there are no beaches there for Sun and surf lovers. The area is largely salt marshes and peat bog.

Salt has been produced here since before the 9th century and even today there are still over 250 workers employed in the industry.

That evening we walked from our hotel into the old walled town and enjoyed a superb meal with great entertainment provided by two young musicians, one of whom, a young girl, sang and played blues guitar and serenaded us into the night as we all sang along.

Inside the walled town of Guerande

The market square and Norman Chrurch

Two towers at the entrance illuminated by a changing light show.

A man walking his Donkey

Day 5

Originally, I had hoped to follow the coastline all the way down from Guerande to Royan, however, on close inspection of the map realised that this would be impossible. We were resigned to using the motorway system much more than I had wanted to as we made our way to Royan. On the way, we drove through St-Nazaire, skirted around Nantes, bypassed La Roche, La Rochelle and then finally Rochefort. Not knowing what wonders, we may have seen if only we had more time to stop.

Once we had arrived in Royan we were uplifted by the sight of a magnificent sea view. The beaches are superb and we found our hotel with ease as it was located prominently overlooking the North beach and promenade. There we were greeted by our English-speaking host and shown to our room which was at the base of the building and facing a sea view. The room had recently been refurbished and was unusually, accessed via some double-glazed doors adorned with shutters on the outside. I suppose they were like seaside chalets, and you can't get any more French than that. I was delighted and felt I had made a good choice.

The weather was still hot and sunny and my wife decided to have a paddle in the sea as soon as we were able to unpack and walk out. I, sensibly, found a bar overlooking the sea front and enjoyed a cool beer, or two.

My wife was pleasantly surprised by how warm the water was, especially in the knowledge that Royan is in the middle of the Bay of Biscay and Atlantic waves arrive there directly from America.

This stretch of coastline is a great favorite for surfers but when we were there the sea was unusually flat calm. We explored the promenade in both directions from the hotel and looked admiringly at the expensive houses and hotels which overlooked the sandy bays. Finally that evening we had our evening meal at a restaurant overlooking the beach and watched the sun go down. As the darkness set in we were treat to a laser light display which lit up the sand on the beach and also the rocks to the North, where little fishing huts hung, clinging on to the cliffs and were illuminated by the assorted colours of the light.

The North Bay at Royan

A Carrelet used for fishing

In this area of Charante Maritime you can see curious little fishing huts called Carrelets overhanging the cliffs. This method of fishing dates to the 14th century where a square net is lowered into the water at high tide using a hand operated winch and pulled up at the appropriate time when a fish or two might be caught in the net. Some owners use bait to entice the fish and so probably attract the odd crustacean also.   We had been in the Sun that long I was beginning to feel like a crustacean myself.

The next sandy bay to the south

Looking across the bay to the North

A beach at Royan with our hotel seen in the top left

Day 6

We left Royan in the morning after a late breakfast and for the first few kilometers hugged the beach front. Partly to see the beaches and promenades, which were both fabulous, but also to have a quick peek at the 'International Frisbee competition' which was being held there that week. 1200 competitors from 30 nations throwing Frisbee's. At each other. We were very surprised to see the magnitude of the event but not surprised to see that it had made parking the Honda nearby almost impossible, so we went on our way much the wiser…. Wondering, where were all the dogs?

By this time, we were getting very close to our next destination. A small hamlet called Saint Romain, not far from the village of Aubeterre where we had decided to base ourselves for a few days where we could explore the Dordogne.

We Looked at the map and noticed we were not too far from the famous town of Cognac. So, drawn by the glamor and the brand, decided to go there first and fill in some of the day. I drove the Honda directly into the center of town, as I always did when exploring towns, but seemed to ricochet back out again having not seen anything interesting at all to look at. I did a second pass, drove down off the bridge and along the riverside, and up past the Cognac distillery looking for somewhere to park, so we could walk a while and perhaps grab a coffee or even visit the distillery. Unfortunately, we were unable to find the entrance to the distillery and decided that Cognac was not worth spending any more time in and left.

The Cognac distillery is bang in the middle of the town but seemed to be crowded on all sides by narrow streets and buildings. Parking seemed to be a big problem in the town, so after witnessing a driver shunt another car in order to get parked, in a ridiculously small space, and me being eager to get to our base camp, we left Cognac accepting that we may well have missed something of great interest. Not to mention some cheap Brandy!

As we drove from Cognac the landscape had changed and we were surrounded by field after field of grape vines. Fields meticulously planted with perfectly trimmed vines as far as the eye could see. Cognac had certainly made its agricultural presence in this part of France, no mistaking.

Grapes by the hectare near Cognac

A note about French drivers

Before I comment on French Drivers, and I can only generalise about this, during our time in France we found the French people extremely friendly, courteous and helpful. I speak very little French but can apologise for my limited understanding of French, in French, and that with a few words seemed to be enough for them to want to gladly help me out. It is important etiquette to always greet the owner of a shop, or when meeting people generally, with a big smile and a Bonjour, and you will be well on your way to being rewarded with a friendly encounter.

S'il Vouse Plait, French Drivers, as I see them.

There are strict driving regulations in France as there are in all civilised countries. However, in France drivers seem to interpret them differently to we English drivers. Speed limits are posted everywhere and are as follows: - 130kmh Motorways, 110kmh Dual Carriageways, 90km on country roads, reducing to 70km, 50km and even 30km in areas where pedestrians are liable to be close by.

In the UK these are regarded as maximum speed limits. NOT IN FRANCE. In France, posted speed limits are in fact TARGETS. You must achieve the speed limit without haste and be at least on or slightly over, just to keep in harmony with them.

French drivers also habitually tailgate the car in front, it seems to be compulsory, so, you always travel with close company. You can be on a stretch of road with no traffic for miles in either direction but have one French driver behind you and it will be about four meters from your rear bumper.

On one occasion, when leaving a 50 zone into a 70 zone I was cruising along admiring the landscape and only managed to climb to a steady speed 56kmph. I looked in my rear-view mirror to see an irate middle aged lady in the car behind waving her arms around as if to say what the **** are you playing at? Get moving! This is something you must come to terms with because it happens ALL THE TIME.

French drivers must be trained from inception to drive this way, having not the slightest fear of collision. So, either Hit the speed target or slightly over, or get off the road. Although, even that is not quite as simple as you might think! Why? Because in France it is Law that if you see a vehicle broken down you must stop to offer your assistance. So, pulling over to let your tail chaser past, can be somewhat confusing, for an old lady that's been clinging onto your shirt tails since the last roundabout.

It should be noted that most old ladies who drive in France assume the accolade of being Alan Prost no less. And they can go like stink! Therefore, no quarter is given to the British tourist in his classic sports convertible. Even with a GB sign prominently displayed on the boot. That said, if you are looking for a race, here is the place to do it. The roads are amazing, but more of that later.   This now brings me to my next and penultimate criticism of French Drivers. French Drivers always want to straighten out the bend and take the racing line, which, when you are passenger in a right-hand drive car on the wrong side of the road and the approaching vehicle is one foot over the dotted line and on your side in a bend, can be somewhat disconcerting, especially for the passenger, as got pointed out to me several times by my wife.

Parking

Parking in Paris is a contact sport.   What can you say?

Day 7

On-route to Saint Romain we passed through a small town called Chalais where we stopped at the local supermarket to buy enough food and drinks to last us through the first few days. Chalais has two supermarkets including a Lidle. There is also a Market held there every week, as in most French towns.

Eventually we arrived at our destination in Saint Romain. We had telephoned our hosts in advance so they were prepared for our arrival and welcomed us with a bottle of wine, some bread and a selection of jams. No points for guessing which got devoured first. The owners Carole and Richard made us feel very welcome, the location was better than we had expected and the Gite was great with a large swimming pool for us to use to cool off in. Base Camp was sorted. I felt that for the first time on the trip and I was able to relax, take stock and update my journal. We were also introduced to Morgan the Cat, whom, over our period at the Gite became a regular visitor and proved to be a good companion when I was writing or just having a late lie in.

Morgan the Cat

Base Camp Saint Romain. The old Schoolhouse Gite.

So far, the weather had been fabulous, however, the forecast ahead looked somewhat dubious and we needed to plan our time, taking this into consideration. Two places we had both wanted to visit in the Dordogne area were Brantome and Sarlat-La-Caneda. Sarlat was the furthest away so we decided to make for there first. Before the weather changed!

Authors Note

When I decided to write this account of our trip, I did not want to recite Road number after road number expecting that one day someone might follow blindly in every step we had taken, as I have seen others do. Sometimes it's fun to get lost a bit and go off the map, as you never know what you might discover. Sometimes I would ignore the navigator and just deliberately deviate from a rout and do a bit of exploring. However, I am going to make one exception on this occasion, because, when we drove to Sarlat I encountered two roads that you must drive if you decide to come anywhere near here. The D47 from La Douze to Sarlat and also the D32.

Any spirited Honda S2000 driver will tell you that the Honda S2000 with stock does not handle well on bumpy and undulating roads. It can get right out of shape, making for a real white knuckle ride. Especially as the S2000 is so light. Not so here. These two roads are as smooth as silk, with bends that the Honda just eats up. Silverstone would be proud to own such a stretch of highway. Fast, clear roads with little or no traffic and with bends of every dimension that make driving such a pleasure. It also made me wish I was riding my old Moto Guzzi, for a while. (Gone are the days unfortunately). It must be said that there are so many roads in this part of France that are just superb for driving and make our roads look poor by comparison. The verges and hedgerows are also immaculately trimmed making the scenery and the drive even better. Its not hard to see where a lot of French taxation is spent.

Day 8

It was a Saturday, so when we arrived in Sarlat it was market day and the town was jumping. Yet again, it was another fine sunny day when we cruised into the town with the top down. Taking a chance, I drove straight into the center where a roundabout marked the Northern end of the market and on a piece of waste ground nearby just as we arrived another car was pulling out to leave, so we found a good space for the S2000 under the shade of a tree.

The market at Sarlat is a true spectacle. It occupies the main central area of the town and must be half a kilometer in length with offshoots into every nook and cranny either side and includes a covered in section where you can find food items such as cheeses, cooked meats and homemade macaroons. There are dozens of restaurants, Ice cream parlors and the usual high Street boutiques. Wandering outside of the market area, Sarlat has a very old church, a park and water gardens that make for a great day out with plenty of variety. We ate lunch in a restaurant next to the church and did a bit of people watching until eventually the traders started to disassemble their stalls in the afternoon sun.

Homemade Macaroons

People watching from the restaurant in Sarlat

A short walk away from the center of Sarlat, peace.

   After lunch in Sarlat we headed north to explore another small town my wife had read about called Montignac. This proved to be a great find as Montignc is located on the V'eze're river and is a good spot to take a canoe trip or just sit at one of the restaurants on the bank side and watch the river trickle by. Nearby are the famous Lascaux caves which were discovered in 1940 and are adorned with pre-historic paintings. The caves are such an important archeological discovery they have been totally recreated to preserve the paintings in the original cave. I parked by the riverside and we began walking a route through the town and over each of the two bridges, eventually bringing us full circle.

A view between the two bridges of Montignac

The Local Cinema?

By the river at Montignac

Day 9

Another spectacularly beautiful town located in the North of the Dordogne region is the pretty village of Brantome. I first came across Brantome by accident on Google Earth when looking at a French property website. Brantome sits on the oxbow of the river Dronne with sheer cliffs to the North which form a splendid back drop to a very picturesque Benedictine Abbey built by Charlemagne in 769. The architecture on the bridges, the restaurants that overlook the river and the old waterwheel are a photographer's dream. When we arrived, there was a Craft Fair in a park on the South side of the river where you can see huge yew trees that must be hundreds of years old offering welcome shade for the tourist. To the south of the village you will find ample parking for cars and motorhomes as parking is very limited in the village.

Shooting the wear at Brantome

Stuck on the chute

The waterwheel calmly rotates as diners enjoy le déjeuner

View of the river Dronne from the Abbey

Day 10

And so on Monday it rained! But not to be disheartened, we decided to go to the market at Chalais and just get wet. Surprisingly, we met a Yorkshire Woman selling English groceries from her stall to local ex pats who were homesick for those English delicacies you can just never do without. Marmite, Tetleys Tea, Marmalade and Golden Syrup were a few things I can remember seeing on the stall. We had a good chat, but were not so long away from home that we were pining English food just yet. I suggested some Ritz Crackers to go with her peanut butter the next time she went shopping and she thought it was a great idea. Peanut Butter and Ritz Crackers…..mmmmm. Apart from that It was all a very French affair and we even saw some wild Escargots in the raw for sale. Mouthwatering! Yes?

Cheap Snails?

Chalais on market day

That afternoon the weather improved, so we kept on motoring and visited the nearest town to Saint Romain, a pretty village called Aubeterre. Here we would have lunch and visit the 7th century Subterranean Monolithic Church which was hewn out of the solid limestone rock cliff face. The Church of Saint-Jean contains the tomb of François d'Esparbes de Lussan, Marshal of Aubeterre, along with other holy relics.

Subterranean Monolithic Church of Saint-Jean

The gallery of the Church is 15 Meters high

Aubeterre

Entrance to the Church of Saint-Jean

  An artificial beach has been created on the river Dronne at Aubeterre, with a play area for children and you can hire a canoe and paddle the river in either direction. There is also a Motorhome site just by the bridge over the river, a short walk from the town.

  We ate our lunch in the village square under a canopy when it began to rain so we hastily retired to Saint Romain where eventually the sun came out and we were able to enjoy the pool and Morgan's company for a while, before another evening meal at camp. Overall not too busy a day and not such a lot of time behind the wheel for a change.

Day 11

Tuesday, and the weather looked fair. Today we would go for the wine. To St. Emilion we headed. There is no direct route to St Emilion and the Garmin had me off in all directions and driving along the narrowest of roads. I now understand that the French road numbering system can be a problem for satellite navigators, as all roads classified as D roads can be either super wide highways, or, can also be the narrowest of farm tracks. Albeit with tarmac. In the UK we would regard these roads as unclassified. Subsequently, the Garmin thinks it is sending you on the fastest route, but in fact, it could actually be the slowest. Once I had this worked out I headed for the nearest town and used signposts to back up the navigation. Like we used to do in the old days!

As we approached St Emilion the landscape changed and became reminiscent of the day we drove through Cognac. Hectares of fields, supporting thousands of vines planted in neat rows, all perfectly pruned to deliver the best grape harvest. Then the vineyards would appear. More and more as we neared St Emilion. Eventually we arrived in the village of St.Emelion and having done some research, I knew, as so often would be the case, parking would be a problem. However, we managed to find some ground on a bend at the edge of the village and pulled in behind a family unloading their bicycles. It was at this point an age-old problem I had had with the remote locking system on the S2000 reoccurred. I was sure I had repaired the fault with the Hamilton Palmer immobilizer, but here it was back again. The remote access to lock the doors failed to operate. I was still able to lock the doors with my key, but knew I would need to address the problem again at some point when we were back home.

St Emelion is quite a quaint and picturesque village but when you visit some of the up-market shops and see wines on offer at €4000 and more, you soon realise that there is an undertone of bourgeois opulence here that makes this industry more than just agriculture at its finest.

A vineyard as we approached St. Emilion

The main mall at St Emilion

Tourists negate the steep cobbled lane downwards

We followed the tourist trail that took us to several viewpoints where you can gaze over the village and beyond into the countryside, and on this day in particular, could also see the thunder in the clouds that overshadowed the valley below. We decided to lunch in a restaurant which was located on a very steep cobbled street that had only a few tables outside but where we could watch other pilgrims negate the slippery cobbles downwards. Inside the restaurant there were more tables in what seemed to be carved out of the solid rock. While we ate, the Heavens opened and we gave thanks for the canopy above us where prior to the rain a cat had been stretched out napping. It was in this restaurant I enjoyed the best meal I had eaten so far in the time we have been in France. It was not as expensive as some meals we have eaten and the service was excellent.

St Emilion

I think the one on the bottom right has its skirt lifted just above the knee!

After lunch, we called in to the tourist information service to find out where we could visit a vineyard. We were suitably directed to a Vineyard called Champion, not far to the North and roughly in the direction we would be travelling on our way back to Saint Romain. The suggestion sounded 'Champion' to me and so on we went post-haste. Unfortunately, we were to arrive at the Champion Vineyard half way through a FREE English guided Tour, but very fortunately arrived there just in time for the wine tasting part. This of course being the most important.

The tasting room at Champion

    Having sniffed, sloshed and spat out three or four times, we conceded to learning little from the experience, except (and I thought this was very interesting) why the growers plant roses at the edges of the vines. It's fascinating to know that they use the roses to detect pests as they are more vulnerable than the vines and so act as an early warning system for when to spray.

    We purchased three bottles of wine, all much more expensive than the ones we acquired from Lidle, and one, more expensive than anything I have ever purchased before, ever. At €14.50 for a 2012 Vintage, and which did not impress me very much at all at the tasting but which I reluctantly took advice on. I looked the brand up when we returned home and found them available in the UK for £12 bottle. I must trust my instincts more often!

Discount Monsieur?

Roses detect pests before the vines become susceptible

Wine tasting

Day 12

Sadly, the time came to say goodbye to our hosts Carole, Richard and Morgan the cat. Morgan appeared at the front door soon after we were up that morning and as we packed our picnic lunch she finished off the last of the Parma ham and some cream left over from a flan desert the night before.

Loyalty in cats can only be measured by the next meal you give them, so in true Cat form, she was nowhere to be seen when we were ready to drive off. I wasn't upset! I wasn't!

Back on the hotel trail and heading North again the road took us to Confolens. A small but very pretty town, again on the Vienne river. We arrived in town and parked the Honda but elected to sit for a while and wait until a rain cloud passed over. Then we did the usual investigation around the key parts of the town. It seems we had developed a pattern to our exploring. Market square, church, bridge, then anything other of special interest. We crossed the foot bridge over the river to take pictures and then made a circuit of the North side of town which proved to be relatively uninteresting, returning by way of the riverside. It was here we passed by a cottage where a gentleman was pottering in his garden and in true Geordie style my wife struck up a conversation. Steve, and his wife Maddy, had bought the cottage at the bridge end as a holiday home and were pleased to show us around their property. while we sat drinking coffee a storm erupted and it rained so heavy Steve and Maddy kindly invited indoors until the storm eventually passed. Big thank you to Steve and Maddy. Someday we'll meet again!

We left Steve and Maddy to conclude our spin around the town and discovered a British Fish and Chip shop, of all things, just over another bridge on the river. Confolens has a large British ex-pat community so this has been a very popular attraction for both visitors and locals alike. We bought some chips to complement our picnic and then set off for Montmorillon, another town on the river Vienne, a little further to the North.

Confolens

Confolens

Saint-Germain-de-Confolens

Montmorillon

   Montmorillon is famous as a place renowned for writing. There is a typewriter museum in town, along with a museum dedicated to the not so humble Macaroon. It is also well known for the discovery of a clay substance named after the village called Montmorillonite which has many uses as it contains several trace elements that are advantageous towards having a healthy body.

   Again, Montmorillon is another French village where you find stunning views from the river, especially near to, or on the bridge.

Montmorillon

Montmorillon

Montmorillon

  We completed our investigation of Montmorillon and as the weather showed some improvement decided to put the top down for the drive to our next hotel, located adjacent to a golf course and near the town of Beauvoir, just a few kilometers South of Poitiers.

  Garrigae Manoir de Beauvoir was a converted country house, not quite a chateau, but very pleasant all the same. The golf course extends South from the hotel and there is a splendid club house and a driving range. There is also a fitness club and outdoor swimming pool here, unfortunately the pool had been covered when we were there due to the inclement weather.

Garrigae Manoir de Beauvoir

I took some time out to try and locate the problem with the Honda's remote door locking mechanism. Having pulled down the Hamilton Palmer remote entry control box which is located under the dashboard. I began to fiddle. I was already familiar with the unit as this is where I had traced the door locking problem to originally. The box contains two relays mounted onto a circuit board. In this case both relays seemed to be responding to the alarm remote fob OK, but yet the doors would still not lock. Then by accident, I bent one of the two triac's attached to the board which stands proud on its 3 legs, and BINGO, the doors started locking again. It seems the soldered joints on the circuit board have been failing with age. I may need to re-solder these again as a precaution.

Hotel Garrigae Manoir de Beauvoir boasted a very fine restaurant and for the first time on our adventure in France we actually experienced what had so far eluded us, "French Cuisine" complimented by some nice Rose wine. We ate our very fine meal and I proudly celebrated my success in repairing the Honda's remote access mechanism.

Overlooking the pond and golf course at Garrigae Manoir de Beauvoir

Day 13

We breakfasted at Garrigae Manoir de Beauvoir and set off heading North again, time this time for the beautiful Chateau Azay-le-Rideau. En-route, the road surface seemed to change to that of a patchwork quilt of repairs and uneven bumpy surfaces. Totally unlike what we had been experiencing further south in France. This proved to be somewhat disappointing for driving and it continued like that all the way to Richelieu. We stopped at Richelieu for a break and walked the gardens and visited the petit Chateau, where inside there is a model and picture of the chateau before it was dismantled in 1805.

The chateau had originally been built by the Cardinal Richelieu before his death in 1642. We decided to call into the tourist information to get the story surrounding the demise of the Chateau as my recollection of Cardinal Richelieu came only from Alexandre Dumas "Three Musketeers". Richelieu was Louis XIII's Chief Minister.

It was here I was made aware of a classic car rally taking place over a three-day period in the town of Montbazon, just south of Tours and not too far off our planned route.

On arriving at Montbazon we tried unsuccessfully to find the classic cars ourselves, crisscrossing the town several times, but then gave up and went to the tourist information office. The lady there was not much help, even when I showed her the leaflet given me in Richelieu about the event. So again, concerned about the lack of time pressed on to Chateau Azay-le-Rideau.

The monument to Cardinal Richelieu

Views in the Park at Richelieu

Entrance to the square at Richelieu

A water fountain in the square at Richelieu.

The Peti Chateau located in the park at Richelieu

Chateau Azay-le-Rideau.

The now state owned Chateau is an icon of the new art of 16th century building in the Loire Valley. The Chateau is located on an island in the river surrounded by the beautiful village of the same name and is currently enjoying a €5.3 million refurbishment. Unfortunately, because of the work in progress we were unable to go inside. However, due to the time constraints we were under I was happy to take photographs from outside, have coffee in the converted washing house in the garden and take a tour of the lovely village. Eager to get to our next destination point.

Entrance to the Chateau Azay-le-Rideau

The village square

Our next stop is quite famous in the world of Motorsport and was a key factor in determining our planned route North. Hotel de France, located in Chartre-Sur-le-Loir and is famous for hosting the racing drivers and their cars that would go to Le Mans to compete in the 24-Hour race. The place is steeped in racing history and the bar is decorated with photographs of famous drivers such as Graham Hill and Sir Stirling Moss.

   We drank cold beer outside the hotel and watched as classic cars drove past in the evening sunshine.

   Food at the Hotel De France is superb and plenty. We were quite amazed at the quality and quantity of food which included a free cheese course before desert. Regrettably we declined the cheese as knew we could not manage both.

Hotel De France

Day 14

It was raining again when we checked out of Hotel de France, but fortunately the S2000 was parked half under cover so I could load the boot in the dry. By now, I had repacked the boot that many times I had it down to a fine art. There was hardly an inch of space left when I closed the boot lid. I drove out of the garage, around the square and reversed up the lane that divided the annexed bedrooms with the main building. This had been the site of many photo shoots over the years when the Aston Martin racing team would stay here with their cars, prepared to do the 24-hour race at Le Mans. There is even a photograph with Sir Stirling Moss standing here, so I knew I was standing on hallowed ground when I took this photograph of the S2000 before we too Went to Le Mans.

Hotel De France   Chartre-Sur-le-Loir   Honda S2000

We arrived at the racetrack in Le Mans in the wet, fulfilling a premonition I had been having for some time about this day. To get into the museum you must ignore google and head for the main entrance. Car parking is up a narrow lane to the left behind the building. We parked in an almost empty car park but not before taking another photograph of the S2000 outside the main entrance. Parking is up the lane past the white van in the center of the picture. If you are interested in racing cars, then this is a great place to be. The museum was very quiet and so we moved quickly and quietly between exhibits clicking merrily away with my camera. I purchased tickets that allowed us access to the track but the weather determined we had a very brief view of the circuit before heading for cover inside to look at the exhibits. The 24hr race also uses some of the roads outside the track for normal traffic. It could be said then that we drove the Honda S2000 on the Le Mans 24HR Racing Track! As well as the excellent museum, there is also a very smart gift shop here, where we purchased some branded presents for our two grown up sons.

Le Mans Racing Circuit

Le Mans Racing Circuit

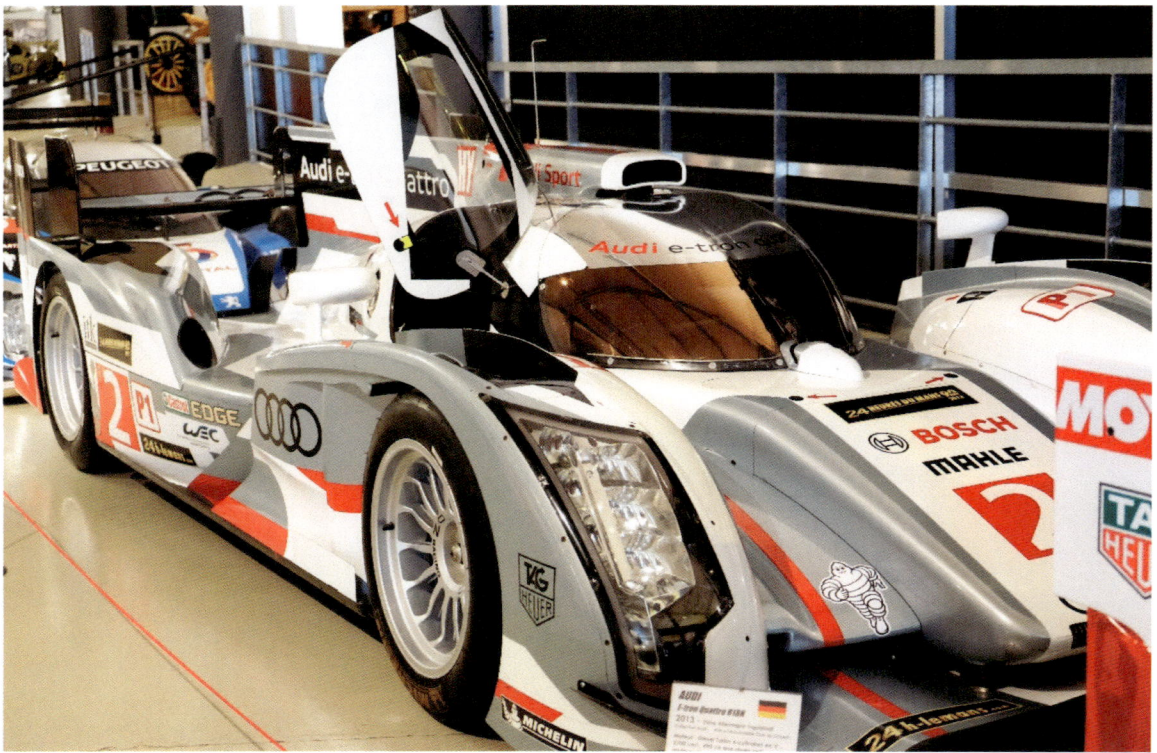

Examples of the exhibits Inside the Museum

A huge collection of miniature sports cars.

   Another box ticked, it was time to head North again and as we had plenty of time this day, decided to drive into Chartres. Our hotel (Chateau) that evening was located just North of Chartres and by lunchtime the weather had improved nicely. Once again, we could not find anywhere to park in Chartres and after heading for the Cathedral were disappointed that Chartres seemed to be such a busy commercial center. The roads we drove on in town were also atrocious, with many having man hole covers every few feet. They say people living in Paris come to Chartres for week end breaks, but having spent a week in Paris myself cannot for the life of me see why they would leave Paris to come here. We probably missed the best of Chartres, as I expect we had probably done in Cognac.

   Having given up on Chartres we headed back out into the countryside and found another great road heading to our planned destination of the day in a place called Denonville. A sleepy hamlet in the middle of nowhere, Denonville is dominated by an old Chateau built in the 17th century by Jacques Rene De BRISAY who was Couverneur of CANADA 1685-1689 and is now used as a place for hosting weddings as well as a B&B.

We were in an annex off the main building, in a period room which retained most of its original features. Unfortunately, there was no restaurant at Denonville but we were informed that there was several in the local village. Unfortunately, we had to drive Nine kilometers to get there.   Auneau is a pretty village where we found a choice of restaurants located around the main square. It's surprising that the local supermarket and patisseries were open until 7.00pm in such a small village.

The road through Auneau is pot ridden and proved to be a very bumpy ride in the S2000, even though we had emptied the boot of all our luggage. We ate at an Italian styled restaurant and so I had my old favorite, Spaghetti Bolognaise. I asked for some Garlic Bread as I knew that would really make me feel at home, but unbelievably the owner said she did not know of such a thing. At that point I frantically conferred with the app in my phone to seek out the French translation for "You Have Got To Be Kidding Me" but ended up bemused and totally disappointed.   No Garlic Bread?

Chateau De Denonville

An old van outside the Marie's office in Denonville

Day 15

Breakfast at Chateau Denonville was a strange affair as everyone sat around the same large oval table. I was hoping to run the S2000 around to the front of the Chateau to take a picture but two catering vans turned up while we were having breakfast and blocked the driveway. So very disgruntled we left for **Versailles**.

The weather deteriorated even further this morning and as we neared Versailles the traffic became more intense, it was a Saturday after all. I decided that I could do with a day off touring so we headed straight for the Novotel Hotel, not too far from the Palace of Versailles. The hotel is located on a roundabout on the main road that leads to the palace and has an underground car park. Take the exit to the right of the hotel building should you go there and the ramp for the car park is immediately on the left. The security gate for the entrance was closed but a phone call to reception had the electric doors open and I parked the S2000 Safe and secure.

On Saturday evenings during the summer months the Palace holds a "Fountains and Fireworks" display. I had already ordered tickets and this was to be the highlight of the evening. In the afternoon, we went shopping in Versailles and we enjoyed a posh, French-style coffee in a MacDonald's that sold French pastries and fresh coffee. That evening we ate at the Novotel and decided to take a taxi down to the palace to save our now aching feet but would walk back to the hotel. Although we had seen the Palace of Versailles before it had been in January, so we had not actually seen the fountains working. This night would prove to be a real spectacle as the sky cleared and we watched the fountains and Fireworks against another gorgeous setting Sun.

The entrance to the Palace

The fountains inside the palace gardens

Orchestrated Prelude to the Fireworks

A Sunset at the Palace of Versailles

Day 16

Throughout the whole journey in France I had avoided the toll road system but always knew there was a chance we may need to use it on our way from Versailles to Le Havre. As it turned out I ended up having no choice. The plan was to drive down to the Palace after leaving the hotel, park outside the palace on a paved area at the front and take a picture of the S2000. I thought I knew the way, having walked it already, but managed to completely botched it. We headed for the palace and then mysteriously got sling shot out of Versailles onto the A14 heading toward Paris. The Garmin suffered terribly as we found ourselves in a network of underground tunnels and unable to get our bearings. We seemed to be always going in the wrong direction and then suddenly, I drove around a bend and there it was, the dreaded toll booth. We were unable to turn around and therefore had to put some euros in the machine where the barrier lifted and we were the opposite. Then, given a choice of two roads, I was forced to stop in the middle of the divide and put my hazards on while we took time to navigate. Eventually we picked a rout that finally gave us signs for Le Havre and Rouen. But on a toll road.

In total, we were to pay approximately £30 in tolls at a series of booths from Versailles to Le Havre. Expensive motoring! Nevertheless, we made Le Havre in plenty of time to have another MacDonald's and chat to some fellow Brits in the same queue for the ferry. We also found time to walk into the shopping mall along the harbour and take in the regeneration of the old dock area.

Once the terminal gates opened at 3.00pm we picked up our boarding passes and formed up in a queue behind the Motorhome in front. One of the port operators, a pretty young lady in hi viz uniform came over on my wife's side to ask if the S2000 would make the ramp because she thought it may be too low. I leaned over to speak to her as she leaned in to the open window and accidentally put my elbow on the headlight washer button, giving her the shower of her life. The whole thing was quite embarrassing but eventually we all saw the funny side once she had gone to dry off.

Once on board the ferry I found myself parked in front of a classic American Ford Mustang. This same car had been at The Hotel De France when we were there and I had taken a photograph of the hotel with the Mustang parked nearby and in shot. So, we had a good chat with the owners and later sent them the picture.

The trip back to Portsmouth was uneventful and we tried hopelessly to get some sleep in our cabin. We also ate on board in the knowledge that it would be very late when we checked in at the Langstone, where we eventually arrived at about 10.15pm. As we drove into the car park at the Hotel, a family from Sweden came out to greet us? The head of the family expressed his delight at seeing the S2000 and told me that he also owns an S2000 back home in Sweden. He and his family had been to the festival of speed at Goodwood and were on their way home the following day. I have never met anyone so enthusiastic about the Honda S2000. So, we chatted and chatted until eventually they went off to bed and we could go to the bar. I like bars. The next day we would stay with an old friend of mine who lives in Winchester before making the long journey home to Durham.

Summary

The Honda coped extremely well with the journey and better for having done some long runs. Driving with the top down through France is the best driving experience you can ever imagine and I encourage anyone to do the same. France is beautiful and I can't wait to begin planning another adventure in the Honda S2000. This was probably the longest trip the car had made in its 17years and 52,000miles. And possibly mine too.

During the trip, we logged 3,858 kilometers.

Top Down Most of The Way

Printed in Great Britain
by Amazon